Fireflies

Written by Lucy Floyd

Celebration Press

Parsippany, New Jersey

Lights dance in the summer sky. What are they? Fireflies!

Another name for this little insect is lightning bug.

Male fireflies blink in mid-air.

Female fireflies blink
on leaves.

Fireflies use their lights to send
messages to each other.

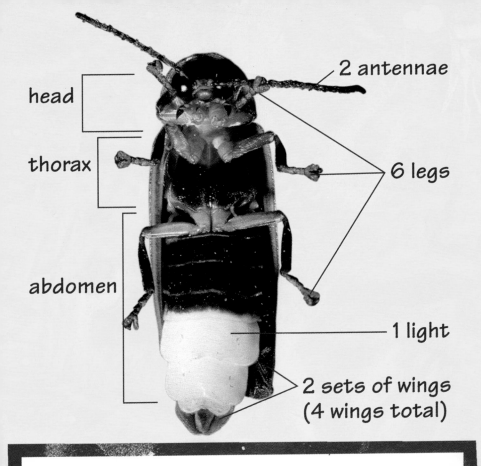

head

thorax

abdomen

2 antennae

6 legs

1 light

2 sets of wings
(4 wings total)

Like all insects, they have
six legs.

Firefly Larva

Firefly Eggs

Female fireflies lay eggs.
A larva hatches from the egg.
A larva is a baby firefly.
The larva turns into a pupa.

Firefly Pupa

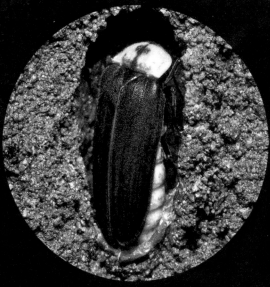

Adult Firefly

The pupa turns into an
adult firefly.
It takes about two years for an
egg to grow into a firefly!

Lights dance in the summer sky.
Fireflies!